TEXT HIM This NOT That

By Gregg Michaelsen

**Texting Tips to Build Attraction
& Shorten His Response Time!**

DISCLAIMER: As a male dating coach I am very good at what I do because of my years of studying the nuances of interpersonal relationships. I have helped thousands of women understand men. That said, I am not a psychologist, doctor or licensed professional. So do not use my advice as a substitute if you need professional help.

Women tell me how much I have helped them and I truly hope that I can HELP you too in your pursuit of that extraordinary man! I will provide you with powerful tools. YOU need to bring me your willingness to listen and CHANGE!

ISBN: 978-1-7222-8078-9 (paperback)

Contents

Introduction

TEXTING TIPS TO BUILD ATTRACTION and SHORTEN HIS RESPONSE TIME!

Let's face it, texting is the way in which most of us communicate on a daily basis. It's in the workplace, our 80-year-old parents and grandparents are texting and kids know how to text at an early age. It has all but replaced face-to-face interactions for the most basic types of communication.

Research tells us that 44% of men and 37% of women find texting to be an easier way to flirt and get acquainted with a new love interest. Roughly one-third of men and women believe it is less intimidating to ask for a date via text than on the phone. Probably because it's less painful if you get shot down.

Across all age groups from 21-50, roughly one-third of all surveyed said they use their mobile device to schedule and plan dates. Texting is definitely part of the dating world for both men and women!

While there are differences in how we text, depending on how old we are, there are greater differences in the way men and women text, regardless of age. My first texting best seller, *Power Texting Men*, was written to address the texting needs of a younger crowd – women just out of college into their twenties who are looking for a great man.

Text Him This Not That is different. I wrote this book for the more mature crowd, regardless of age. This read is written for women who are less interested in blatant flirting and more interested in using texting to hook a guy and keep him interested!

It is probably no secret to you that men and women are vastly different in how we communicate. Women write me all the time, frustrated with the brief snippets of communication they receive from a man, whether it's in a text or email. What most women fail to understand is that this is how men talk. Think about your past conversations with men. Who does most of the talking? Usually you, right?

This begins as soon as children learn to talk and play together. Boys can be found bumping elbows in the sandbox trying to get the best Tonka Truck available. They communicate with sand in the eyes and punches - not talking and touching hair.

Through actions, not words, are how guys communicate. If I had smartphone at age four, I would whip it to get my point across. There would be no text!

By the time they reach school age, their speech development is usually not as advanced as the girls who have spent every waking moment since they were able, communicating with other little girls with words.

Boys grunt and rub elbows, girls talk. Nothing changes as we get older. I'm going to teach you how to draw him out with texts that he won't be able to resist, just like his boy buds can!

This book isn't just about learning how to text, it's about successfully building a great relationship, using texting as one of the tools in your arsenal. It starts with one element necessary in every great relationship – your ability to challenge one another and build attraction through mystery and intrigue.

That is your best use of texting in your relationship and throughout this book, I will show you many ways in which you can do just that.

To learn the importance of building attraction through mystery and intrigue in your relationship, download my **FREE SPECIAL REPORT:** *Catch Me If You Can!*

Men are wired for the chase. It's part of the excitement of being in a relationship. Part of that chase occurs when the woman plays her most important card – the *catch me if you can* card. A man cannot resist this taunt and unless he's brain dead, he *will* respond.

Your job is to play that card skillfully and in a timely manner. You don't want to use it *all* of the time, but in those moments where it can be most effective. You need to build balance into your texting, just as you do in your relationship as a whole. Too much texting leads to unhappiness and a lack of fulfillment. Too little communication of any sort shows disinterest and leads you to an ultimate end.

When you build challenge and mystery into your texting, you engage his desire to chase you. You build attraction and keep him intrigued. He will always want to know more. He will be salivating in anticipation of your next date. All you need to do is stay one step ahead of him in your texts and he won't know what hit him.

Along with challenge and balance, a good relationship has mutual respect. This can be the first thing you lose in your texting if you aren't careful. Many women lose a guy by texting something too flirty too soon, by appearing to be too needy or by injecting their emotions into the texting conversation.

If you always remember to keep things light and fun, you won't have this problem. Flirting in a text is great, if you know how to do it. Texting should be an enhancement to your relationship, not the primary form of communication.

If you use texting to create that mystery and challenge, to keep him intrigued and interested, your relationship will grow and blossom but if you use it as a tool to deliver your anger, frustration and insecurity, it will be the tool of death for your relationship.

I'm here to help you avoid making those mistakes!

I have chapter after chapter of information included to help you know what men like to see and what they definitely do **not** want to see in a text. I've got all of the major texting blunders most women make and how to avoid them. I will even try to help you revive a relationship damaged by a bad text. Sometimes it's possible, sometimes it's not.

Inside *Text Him This Not That* is not just how to formulate a great text but how to understand the male mind. This is as much about learning how his mind works as it is about learning how to formulate texts he can't resist. How can you communicate with him if you don't understand what he's looking for?

No longer will you be frustrated when you are forced to wait an hour, two hours or even a day for a response. Your days of getting angry because he didn't reply to your last message are over. You will learn the value of having a life outside of *life with your boyfriend* and how to leverage that when you text.

You need to understand a few things about texting before we move on. First and foremost, texting isn't going anywhere any time soon. Yes, we can all remember back to the days where you picked up the phone and called someone but let's face it, those days are gone. We communicate through our thumbs and tiny devices now.

Secondly, there are definite advantages and disadvantages to using texting in your relationship. I will review those with you so you can avoid the disadvantageous texts and use the advantageous ones to build that attraction!

Next, understand one key fact – men are just as nervous as you are in relationships and they are just as afraid as you are to mess things up. He is second-guessing whether or not to send that request for a date Friday night as much as you are. While he may be more to-the-point, he is still nervous and he's sweating your response!

Chapter 1

A QUICK PRIMER

As a woman, you have a built-in ability to be charming. You deliver a look or you use a certain tone of voice and you're able to work your way with men. In an instant, you can melt a man's heart.

When you meet a man you're attracted to, you turn on that charm, you deliver a coy smile, you walk away and he's hooked. Yet, when it comes to texting, you're all thumbs. You're anxious and you feel incompetent. You lose all confidence.

As a result, you text instinctively, like a woman, which is the natural thing for you to do. You can quickly get emotional and frustrated when he doesn't respond as soon as you would like. You might bomb him with texts, getting more worried with each one.

You: I had a great time last night!

Him: *[No response]*

You: Wasn't that fun?

> **Him:** *[2 days later]* I did too! Maybe we can meet up again sometime soon

> **You:** There you are.
> I thought I lost you

All this emotion, anger and frustration is normal. Your flirting skills have evolved over millions of years. Flirting comes as naturally to you as flight to a bird. When you're standing face-to-face with a man, you're good but when you're facing the tiny screen on your phone, you're perplexed.

That's because you expect him to respond like your girlfriends do.

Guy's don't!

Your communication skills also evolved during that time and this new age of emails, texts and carrying our phones with us everywhere has turned us into people who expect, if not demand, immediate responses every time we send something into the cyber-sphere.

This adds to the pressure you're feeling because not only do you expect an immediate response, but you expect to be able to respond equally fast when someone texts you.

What you're not accounting for when you text a man is this:

Men did not evolve!

They still hate talking, regardless of whether it's via text or in person. Men prefer actions as opposed to words. If you would like to learn more about differences between men and women, check out my best seller, *10 Secrets You Need to Know About Men*.

Catch Me If You Can

When you feel confused about what to text a man, just remember this phrase, "*Catch me if you can*". Texting a man with this mindset keeps you focused on sending the right kind of text – a text which creates attraction and desire, mystery and challenge.

Why does this matter? Because when you create attraction, desire, mystery and challenge, you're tweaking all of the strings in your man. This is what men thrive on to keep them interested in you. When you're thinking in this way, you're staying one step ahead of a man.

This also matters because *catch me if you can* means you're not always available as his beck-and-call girl. *This is crucial*. Most women think of this in the opposite way. A man you're interested in texts you for a date the same night and you jump at the opportunity. You're excited and you're afraid that if you don't go, he will dump you.

This is a female line of thinking and, unfortunately, in this instance, it's completely wrong. Being 100% available to a man takes away the challenge for him. He will be more interested in you if you're not always available. When you're texting there are numerous ways to create a sense of being temporarily unavailable. We'll keep touching on this throughout the book.

One way you can create this sense of being unavailable is to tease him in your texts. I don't mean sexting and I don't mean breaking your boundaries. What I mean is laying out the foundation for his mind to go crazy thinking about you.

In this instance the woman is being clever with her answer. She doesn't say yes immediately, instead, she toys with him.

> **Him:** I've got an extra ticket to The Phantom of The Opera next Wednesday; would you like to join me?

> **You:** Depends [*Now leave him hanging for 10 minutes*]

Him: Depends on what? Is that a yes?

You: Depends on whether or not you
can name two of the original songs in
the show

Him: Ah, yeah, hang on
while I google it!

His mind is likely in overdrive at this point, and it's all because you answered in a non-predictable way. You left hanging with the word "depends." He didn't know if you would go or not so he stepped up his game subconsciously. Then you hit him with a fun challenge. Men feel alive when women text them like this.

Successful relationships require some similarities between the partners. This helps build attraction. You and your partner should have similar ways of creating attraction. It's sort of like understanding the language someone speaks. If you're speaking English but he's speaking Latin, you're never going to get very far. The same is true for attraction. If you don't speak the same language of attraction, it won't work.

This similarity extends into other aspects of the relationship like valuing yourself and having a high level of confidence. If you are low confidence and don't value yourself, any relationship you attempt with a high confidence man who does value himself will ultimately fail, and vice versa.

One of your main goals should be to make sure your confidence is high and you value yourself. Without these two things, you will find men who don't value you any more than you do – you will attempt to find happiness and self-worth in your relationships instead of inside yourself.

Every day, I hear from women who tell me they feel very confident in their careers but they feel little confidence in their dating lives. You're not alone if this is how you feel right now.

Bitch Power

I hear this question all of the time, "*Why are men more attracted to the bitchy women instead of the nice ones?*" I'll give you a little hint - it's the same reason women are often attracted to bad boys.

Women often labeled as bitches are the ones who are bold and edgy. They taunt men, they egg men on, they keep men on the edge of their seat. All together, they make for extremely attractive partners!

Him: Meeting a few friends after work for apps. Care to join?

You: Liar. You don't have friends.

Him: I bought a few last weekend.
Hopefully I got a good deal.

Taken by itself, that could be seen as a mean comment. A bitchy comment! But if it's handled with poise, it can be an amazing flirting tool. Good men who aren't overly sensitive love it when women use this in casual conversation. Women are equally challenged when men employ the same tactic.

Nobody wants a "*Yes dear*" partner. Oh, men and women both may act as if that's the type of partner they want, but in reality, if they got that type of partner, they would be bored with the relationship in no time and things would ultimately end badly.

How can you unleash your inner bitch? Let's try one:

Him: How's your day going?

You: Pure hell!

Him: OK, well, maybe I can help?

You: *[No response - ouch! This guy's balls are in a vice after this one!]*

A quality man is attracted to the confidence, bravado and pure sassiness of this conversation. This type of text creates that sense of bitch but in a way that doesn't breed contempt in your relationship. It's edgy but playful – and not responding is part of this edginess.

I hear you now – your mother always taught you that you should seek harmony in your relationships – Mom said not to be a bitch. Now, here I am telling you to go for it. Here's my response to needing harmony in a relationship.

No, no, and NO! **Harmony is boring**! Well, mostly. You want engagement, aggression, passion! When you are using powerful communication tools like those in this book, you are creating a balance. You're not always playing the bitch but you play that card when it seems like you can pull it off. You must learn your partner and be able to read him so you know when it's a good time and when it isn't.

Above, I gave you an example of a sassy text, but how do you temper something that you want to be perceived as sassy and not downright mean? On a little text screen, it isn't always easy to express sarcasm. But that's why they invented smiley faces!

> **You:** I pounded down those fish tacos last night. I think I gained 10!

> **Him:** I noticed. The ocean called and
> wants its fish back!

> **You:** Hey, you were eating so fast you
> choked on that fish bone! ☺

Without the smiley emoticon, that comment could have been taken the wrong way. The exclamation mark helps add a bit of sarcasm and the smiley emoticon lets him know you're not really dumping on his piggish eating habits.

There's plenty more to talk about in regards to emoticons as well as dampeners, as I like to call them. Dampeners are ways to keep a conversation light. Some of these are good, others are actually pitfalls which can sometimes do more damage than good. We'll dig more into both topics throughout.

Some Tips for Building Attraction

The most important thing you need to be aware of in your relationship is this:

YOU set the hidden tempo of the relationship!

What do I mean by hidden? I mean that while a man is expected to be assertive, it's not necessarily because you aren't so yourself. **It's because you let him be.** You know it's important to him that he takes charge and you know that if you let him catch you too early, the relationship won't fully bloom. It is therefore up to you to set the true tempo of the relationship from first date to engagement.

Have you ever heard the saying, *"A man chases a woman until she catches him?"* There is a lot of truth to that statement! Ask any happily married man!

I know as humans, we tend to become impatient and frustrated that we need to engage in what some might call *games*, but the truth is that this type of exchange is necessary to create the required level of attraction – the challenge your man is craving!

A woman's inclination is to nurture – to make another person's life easier by making them feel good when they're down or by boosting them up when they fall. You like to heal things, you don't like to be mean and I know you don't like to play games. I get it. But when texting, this doesn't always work.

> **You:** If you invite me over I will give you a massage.

> **Him:** Really?

> **You:** Yep, and I will put lotion on your
> hands.

This is a very nice gesture and, in the right moment deeper into a relationship, this text is fine, but at the beginning it really doesn't excite a man. He wants to work to get you to do this. You would be much better off teasing him so you get to the date and then just giving him that massage, later, once you know him.

Don't think of this as playing a game – really it isn't. What you're doing is effectively communicating with a man in a way which is meaningful to him and creates the emotions in him you're seeking – interest and attraction!

What you don't want to do is cave in every time he wants something. If you're a confident woman, you have boundaries. If you're going through my *confidence courses,* you will soon establish boundaries. Texting is about establishing and holding onto those boundaries, but in a way which constantly builds respect, not contempt. Don't worry, we'll keep talking about this!

The Sound of Silence

It's not just a great song from Simon and Garfunkel, it's important if you hope to create attraction with your texts! Silence is a powerful tool and can be used to gain the upper hand. The problem with silence is that it is usually something women fear when communicating with a man.

To you, silence means he's ignoring you or he has lost interest or, God forbid, he found something else to do besides talking to you. So, it makes sense that silence directed at him is not only golden, it's your ticket to creating that mystery I mentioned earlier.

When it comes to creating mystery, texting can totally win out over talking on the phone. It may be that in a phone call you'll say too much. With a text, you can be very specific about what you say, and what you don't say.

Here is the golden rule of texting and silence: *the person who texts last is the less mysterious one.* If you don't respond, if you don't comment, you automatically gain the upper hand. You add mystery.

> **Him:** Hey, did I just pass you on Highland Ave?

You: Yep. I saw you. I was applying my lipstick

> **Him:** I slowed down. But you didn't stop. Did you even wave?

> **You:** *[Radio silence]*

Bam! You just knocked this conversation out of the park! I won't even comment on the sassy (and sexy) response to his question. The fact that you left him hanging after his second response makes him want you even more. I can guarantee he's sitting there hoping, no, praying that you text him back. But you're not going to (immediately anyway) because you know better!

Destroy Boredom, Shatter All Things Conventional!

> **You:** So, what's going on with you these days?

> **Him:** Not a lot. Just working, going to school.

I'm going to stop here. I could make that a long text conversation, but I felt repulsed by where it was going. You *do* know where it's going right? To the relationship graveyard! It's going nowhere. There's nothing in that first comment that did anything to build mystery, challenge or attraction into the relationship.

There are two huge mistakes in this short conversation. First, mystery and challenge are simply not created by asking general questions. *How was your day? What are you doing right now? What's the weather like?* These types of statements are not attraction makers, they're attraction killers.

Your goal, when texting a man, is to keep things fun and fresh by using some of the techniques we're discussing. You can't do anything fun or fresh with *"What are you doing right now?"* If a man even bothers to answer this, it's a cursory response and he rolled his eyes as he was typing. In other words, he responded to be nice, not because he's actually interested in the conversation.

Strike one.

The second problem with this exchange is that nobody wants to answer a question like that in a text. Even if you have the most easy-to-use handheld on the planet, you're going to get sick of typing out a response the size of Moby Dick pretty quickly. Keep it simple and stick with precise questions that he can answer without too much trouble.

You want short, fun and challenging interactions. You want to be bold, quirky, and direct! Forget the boring stuff and show him your flirty side. You have tons of time to figure out a response, so relax and wait for it to come to you!

> **You:** How was traffic into Boston this morning? Still woozy from the CO2 fumes?

> **Him:** Haha! Yep. Sucked in fumes for 2 hours.

There we go! This text is focused and you added in a bit of cheekiness as well.

Stick with the Mysterious, Avoid the Vague!

When it comes to men and relationships, mysterious is always good. The more you can make him wonder what you're doing, the better. Mystery is invoked by staying partly aloof. You want him to think you're busy doing lots of fun things, or maybe seeing other interesting people!

> **Him:** What are we doing this weekend darling?

> **You:** Dance class on Friday night. Wine tasting with Jennifer Sat. Crazy busy! Maybe Sunday, I'll let you know.

Do you see what happened? This text creates mystery by avoiding some boring comment like *"Not sure, what are you doing?"* You're obviously busy, and by the sound of it you're meeting people who are **not** him at your dance class. Trust me, he's going to see you as a serious challenge, adding to the attraction.

Responses like these, however, are completely unacceptable:

> Waiting to hear from you.

> I'm up for anything, what do you want to do?

> Kind of tired, long week. What's up?

Similarly, keep ugly vague words out of your texts. Maybe, kind of, perhaps, sort of – they're all too vague! Stick to language that's alive and bold, and you'll become a master at texting in no time.

Give Him Content to Work With. Be a Flirt!

Your goal, when sending texts to a man, is to challenge him. Give him something that he **wants** to respond to. Tease him, mention something he loves or egg him on a little with small comments.

> **You:** It was great meeting your folks last night. Your father is an attractive man! Think he's available?

Him: Just wait 25 years and I'll introduce you to his twin. In the mean time you're stuck with me.

You: Drat! I hate long waits!

Keep poking and prodding him. Get him to smile or laugh and he will love you for it!

You: My parents are in town and they want to meet you. They want to see if you are worth my time and if you are marriage material.

Him: Huh? When?

You: Kidding! They don't even know about you!! 😊

If you want his blood boiling, you can pull the jealousy card. This is a dangerous tool so you need to use it in a measured way, otherwise it could easily backfire. Some guys are going to react to it differently than others. If you've got a geeky guy in your life, steer clear of anything related to jealousy, even in jest.

Here's a great example where it worked:

> **You:** Well crap. I have to hit the gym
> and check out all those buff studs
> again. B.O.R.I.N.G.

> **Him:** Five dollars says I can beat any
> of them at arm wrestling…or at least
> chess.

> **You:** Okay, if you don't hear from me,
> I took a stud home!

The thing that makes these texts okay to do is the **obvious** humor. The B.O.R.I.N.G comment as well as the outright, blatant mention that you will be staring at guys with big muscles is a dead giveaway, or so he thinks, that you aren't interested in doing so. But then, you turn it around and make him jealous when you say your last line…powerful stuff!

Chapter 2

RESPECT

In any successful relationship, there must be respect. Without respect, you ultimately have nothing. To earn respect, whether it's a dating relationship or not, you must set boundaries and hold to them when challenged.

In order to set and maintain boundaries, you need to first respect yourself. If you don't respect yourself, nobody else will either. You become a doormat for people to step on as they see fit. You become the scapegoat for everyone's problems and you're miserable.

Worst of all, you draw in the wrong type of guy – the type of guy who will use and abuse you until he becomes bored with you, then he will dump you and move on to the next woman he finds – another woman just like you. He leaves you in his dust, depleted, dejected and depressed.

When you respect yourself, you don't allow someone to walk all over you. You understand that saying "Yes" to one thing means saying "No" to another. You make the choice on what you will say yes and no to and you hold tight to your decision.

Of course, not all men are like that, but the men who aren't also won't date a woman who doesn't respect herself – at least not for long. Quality men, the men solid relationships are built with, understand the importance of dating women who have a high level of confidence. They welcome learning about your boundaries and would never dream of asking you to change them.

Once you have your confidence where it needs to be, the rest of this becomes easy. You value yourself and you know where those boundaries are. This confidence also enables you to be a challenge to a man, and, as I've mentioned before, this is where you really tweak him and keep him coming back for more!

If you have confidence, then you text men with the same confidence. If you don't have it, you can only fake it for so long. I can't repeat this enough.

As silly as it might sound to you, a man needs to feel he has chased you and he has earned his place in your life. He needs to feel that he has competed and won! This is a key element of the male personality.

Nothing worth having comes without a fight!

By the same token, a man wants a woman who has a lot going for her. Quality men don't want to date women who don't have their act together, financially or otherwise. This tells him you don't value yourself or those things and he does.

Read the conversation below and ask yourself why this woman is not respecting herself, and thus not setting boundaries:

> **Him:** Hey what's up? You doing anything tonight?

> **Her:** No, just watching the news. How about you?

> **Him:** Let's do dinner. Six sound good?

> **Her:** Sure, see you at six!

You may not think there is anything wrong with this conversation. He texted and asked her out – what's wrong with that? Plenty, that's what.

By being immediately available, she lost value in his eyes. A woman who is always available doesn't have a lot going on. This is not challenging to a man. Her attractiveness to him just went down.

You might not think this is a big deal but it is. This guy now expects that she is his beck-and-call girl. Whenever he doesn't have anything to do, he's sure she's available. She just became a rest stop – a woman he will date until his keeper comes along.

If he asked you out at such a late moment, you might be his backup. He might have asked someone else out before you.

You are nobody's backup!

I know what you're thinking – you're thinking that if she turned him down, he would go find another woman. If he does, then he wasn't that interested in her to begin with but if he is a quality man, truly interested in this woman, he will not.

Let's rewrite this conversation in a way that helps her show him she is not his beck-and-call girl.

> **Him:** Hey Susie! How about Chinese tonight? I'm buying!

> **Susie:** Hey! I'd love to, but this is really short notice. Can I get a rain check? How about Sat?

> **Him:** Yeah, sorry. Of course! I'll call
> you on Saturday then. ☺

This is much better for a few reasons. First of all, she had a boundary, which is crucial, but even better, she held her boundary in a friendly way. By starting with *Hey!*, she indicated to him that she was excited to hear from him. That's an immediate ego boost for him. Win!

Next, she offered an alternative – Saturday. This tells him, again, that she's not his beck-and-call girl, but she does want to go out with him.

Perfect. Goal reached.

There is one other biggie in this text – she allows him to finish the conversation. Don't be the last one to talk. Let him end the conversation. No, he isn't always expecting a response. He feels the conversation is over now too and he will drift off into another activity. If you did text him back, odds are he wouldn't respond until later anyway.

Now, obviously, if you are deep into a happy relationship saying yes to last minute dinner request is fine and normal. But, in my example above, I am talking about a relationship in its infancy when setting up boundaries is most important.

It's Never Too Early to Start Building Respect

The time to begin building respect in a relationship is as soon as you meet. If you want to start the relationship off on the right foot and pursue a successful relationship, this is your step 1. To do this, you kindly and in a friendly way establish and maintain your boundaries.

The easiest way to do this is to have a full life outside of your relationship and maintain it after you meet your great guy. Find and pursue hobbies and passions. Find things you want to be involved with and do them. This automatically makes you busy and puts certain boundaries in place. When you *do* meet a great guy, the key is don't give up those hobbies and passions. Many women do this. They give up everything in their life aside from their man. They sit by the phone waiting for him to call while their girlfriends continue to have girl's night out.

Why is all of this so important? First of all, you're busy and this indicates to him you're living a full life. Secondly, he will be interested in learning more about your activities and this stirs mystery. Thirdly, you have those automatic boundaries. You can't see him Thursday night because that's the night you go with your friends to dance class.

A quality man learns that if he wants to rank high in your priorities, he needs to step up his game. This presents him with a challenge. Men need to pursue women. If you're too easy to get, he will quickly move on.

And don't forget the powerful texts you can send him describing your wonderful, exciting life!

> **You:** Whoa! Check out these pics of me zip-lining!
>
> **Him:** You are one crazy-ass woman

See what I mean? Do you really think this guy is going to stop pursuing you? No way with texts like this. This is all because you built a foundation around living a full life and not around some man.

The Power of the Sex Card

Those first few days, and even weeks of a relationship are crucial for respect building. It is important for you to understand that you hold the sex card in the relationship, especially in the beginning. Men can't hold this card. If given the chance, 90 percent of them would have sex with you the minute they meet you.

If you play the sex card correctly, you are guaranteed to drastically increase his interest in you. If you play it too soon, you have essentially told him you don't have boundaries and you don't value yourself. He won't either and he will quickly lose respect for you.

For the same reasons, constant texts with sexual innuendos begin to sound trashy almost immediately. Good men, the men you **want** to date, are quickly going to realize you're not being sexy, but insecure. That was 20-year-old stuff, now you are sophisticated.

FYI: When it comes to sexting, or sending nude photos of yourself via text message, my advice is simple - **don't do it!** Not only do you devalue yourself to a man but you put nude photos of yourself out there for anyone to see. You cannot control what happens once someone receives your photo. He could share them on social media, with his buddies or in any number of ways and before you know it, your reputation is ruined. I get emails from older women who get talked into sexting – don't do it!

Your Approval Doesn't Come From a Man

To text effectively you must understand the importance of having a confident inner game. If you don't, this book becomes useless to you because you can't execute what I teach.

Yes, I know, I beat this point to death!

When you seek approval from a man, you are holding yourself to his values and beliefs, rather than your own. You either don't have your own values or you give them up in lieu of someone else's. Either way, you lose yourself.

Instead of valuing things important to you like honesty and integrity, you value the opinion of someone else. When you receive disapproval, you are devastated, so you work harder to gain the approval of those from whom you seek it. Your own ability to make a decision becomes shadowed by your need for approval. You can no longer make a decision by yourself – you must ask first.

This renders you helpless.

In addition, you give up your own dreams and goals in lieu of the dreams and goals of another. Other negative side effects of seeking approval include:

- Low self-esteem and confidence
- Lower performance levels than you're capable of
- A feeling of not being fulfilled
- Added stress
- Not achieving what you want

Many don't realize they are seeking the approval of others. You might consider yourself to *just be really flexible* and what's wrong with that? Let's look at a few signs of a person who seeks approval:

- Changing your opinion when you realize someone else disapproves

- Giving someone a compliment you don't really mean

- Feeling insulted or worrying about the disapproval of others

- Being afraid to tell someone "No"

- Failing to complain when something isn't right, like a meal you order for example

- Pretending to know something about a subject matter when you really don't

- **Always apologizing** for something you say or do

- Seeking permission when it's not necessary

- Spreading gossip or bad news to gain the attention of others

- Attempting to elicit a compliment from someone or getting upset when someone fails to do so

- Making sure everyone knows you're taking an opposing side to something – you want attention for being the different one

- Doing anything that goes against what you truly believe in because you want to fit in

What if He Leaves?

When you lack confidence, you spend a lot of time worrying about whether or not the guy you've met will leave. As a result, you bend your boundaries and give up on your values in order to try and keep him.

The truth is that in order to keep a great guy, you **must** hold onto your boundaries and values. A good man will respect you for it. A loser will bail and who cares if he does. **Any man who cannot respect your boundaries is not worth your time or energy.** This is something you need to realize and begin to repeat to yourself.

Bringing it All Together: Building Respect through Texting

Now it's time to pull all of this boundary and respect talk into effective texting. How do you do that, you ask? Read on!

Know Your Role!

Men and women both have a role in relationships. Set sexism aside for a moment and hear me out. There are things you do well and things he does well. There are male and female *roles* in dating.

For example, a man needs to be able to take charge. It's how he was raised. You need to allow him to do this. Meanwhile, your role is to lead him without taking charge.

Confused?

No doubt you are because today, women are also being raised to be strong and independent – not to let anyone run over them. I get it and I understand but, if you are the one always asking him out, always planning the dates, always in charge, he will feel emasculated and weak.

Still, as the independent and strong woman I know you can be, there are things you can do to *lead* him to ask you out and plan the date you want.

> **You:** Read this movie review and tell me what you think *[link review]*

> **Him:** It looks awesome. I didn't know it had come out yet!

> **You:** It has! Since we both want to see it we may as well just go together!

> **Him:** Haha…yeah, let's do it. How about Saturday, we'll make it dinner and a movie?

> **You:** You got it mister!

What's good about this conversation? A great thing about it is that it's playful while still getting the job done. This woman wanted him to ask her out to see this movie but she didn't say that, she just tossed the review and other information out there for him to chew on.

She does say, "we may as well go together", which suggests a date but she leaves the actual planning of it to him. He gets to reply with "How about Saturday, we'll make it dinner and a movie", making him feel as if he did the planning and asking.

Is it a trick? Maybe but you get what you want and he gets to maintain his sense of being in charge of things. You and I both know this was really you being in charge, but does he?

Nope!

He walks away thinking he planned everything and is feeling good about himself and you. You're strong and confident and you don't need to be acknowledged as the one in charge.

Men **love** it when women do this. You playfully spring a date on him and you do so in a way that's fun and playful. If he is at all interested, he is going to go on that date with you!

Make the Date His Idea

Here is another example of how to construct a conversation in a way that makes it seem like it's his idea!

> **You:** I just got back from a Chinese buffet with my mom. I think I ate lizard. Kick me if I ever mention going again.

> **Him:** Haha!! That bad huh?

> **You:** It was! The food was poisonous – I grew a tail! Quick, what's the opposite of Chinese food?

> **Him:** I'm going with American food. Final answer.

> **You:** Good, I'm with you! Thursday after work?

> **Him:** Haha, you bet!

Again, this is playful, fun, and witty. No man is going to say no to this! The key for you in initiating these conversations is to remain relaxed and playful. If you make an attempt and he doesn't respond in a way which allows you to continue prompting him for a date, let it go and try again another time. Other opportunities will come

along, or he may even respond later with an idea based
on that conversation.

Chapter 3

NEED

People sometimes can be their own worst enemy. You can become so fixated on getting what you want that you end up pushing it away instead of drawing it closer. We do this because we have unhealthy needs we are trying to meet. This type of need sucks the life out of a relationship. It takes away any attraction and respect that was built early-on. It is usually not something from which you can recover.

You have, no doubt, been on both the giving and receiving end of this unhealthy need. Once it rears its ugly head, the relationship becomes unstable and the balance is shifted too far in one direction or the other. The relationship spirals out of control and ultimately ends in a painful way.

Let's see how need creeps into this texting conversation:

> **Him:** Hey Kim. Slammed at work this week. Can I get a rain check for our date on Tuesday?

> **Her:** Oh c'mon. You've got a better excuse than that I'm sure!

> **Him:** Uh. No. I'm slammed at work.

> **Her:** Whatever. It's fine.

> **Him:** *[No response]*

> **Her:** K. Don't respond then.

This woman sounds needy in an obvious way. If we imagine this relationship to be just a few weeks old, the man is now starting to see her true colors begin to shine through. We can never hide our real selves forever. This guy will most likely give up on this woman. The damage is done.

While her brush-off of his work comment might indicate she doesn't really care, the truth is the opposite. She *needs* him and by postponing their date, she feels as if he is not fulfilling her needs. She might not realize this is why she's reacting as she is, but that's the problem lying beneath the surface.

Initially, she may have been genuine in calling him out on his work statement but she quickly forced things in the wrong direction with her "*Whatever. It's fine*" comment. She ultimately feels he should be setting aside anything and everything to spend time with her regardless of his needs. She has likely done so for him. If I had to guess, I would say that a woman in this instance has already given up her friends, her hobbies and her passions (if she has them) to be 100% available for this guy whenever he calls.

Sadly, this conversation is not uncommon, in fact, it probably continues with more snarky comments from the woman – things like "Oh, are you ignoring me now?" and so on. Meanwhile, *if* he's still looking at his phone, he's rolling his eyes and searching for the block feature.

Rather than assume a man is *just making excuses* not to be with you, assume he is telling the truth. Should you find evidence later that he was lying, deal with it then. Making assumptions, based on your own insecurities, only leads you down a dark and ugly path.

It Goes Beyond the First Few Dates

Unfortunately, this type of problem is not unique to new relationships. It creeps into any relationship and can instantly shift things into an unbalanced situation.

What you need to recognize is that need is different than comfort or intimacy. Need is a codependency thing. You need something about someone in order to feel whole yourself. Maybe you need the security of knowing he is home. Maybe you need him to constantly be validating his love to you. Perhaps you need him to acknowledge the wonderful thing you did for him so you know you're appreciated.

When you do things or say things to force someone to notice you or do something for you, you're expressing an unhealthy need. If your partner is also needy, you two make a dangerous codependent pair, still ultimately doomed to relationship failure.

Having said that, intimacy and comfort are different. Intimacy is built when you and your partner spend *quality* time together. You do something together, like go hiking or see a movie or have a date night, where both of you want to be where you are and you're genuinely enjoying one another's company.

Comfort is providing tenderness and care to someone who is feeling a little down. This can be from the death of a pet or a loved one, from a disappointment like not getting a promotion or new job, or from just having a bad day. You willingly provide this tenderness and care because you deeply care about the other person, not because they manipulated you into doing so.

Texting is just the means to keep the two of you intertwined and excited in-between the actual time spent together.

Controlling the Urge

Need creeps into relationships in all kinds of ways. Some of what we've talked about briefly here may sound a lot like the chapter on approval, and there is definitely some overlap between them. Approval is a specific need you may have but there are others, as I have outlined.

What a lot of this boils down to is keeping your own emotions in check – both the good ones and the negative ones. If you're super in love, you may be riding a real emotional high. Your happy hormones have kicked in and you're riding the wave. These emotions can sometimes be as difficult to control and reign in as negative emotions.

Either way, men don't know what to do with all of those emotions. Women and men express emotion differently, regardless of what emotion it is. Men express love by doing things or fixing things or providing things. Women express love through their words or nurturing. Sadly, they expect men to express their love through words as well.

This is where texting can fail you. Keep your texts short and fun. Use them as a means to keep the attraction going through challenge and mystery until the next date. Save the heavy texting stuff for your girlfriends.

More than one woman has come to me saying, "He never tells me he loves me." When I dig in, I find that he is indeed telling her he loves her by mowing her lawn, fixing her car or changing her oil. He might show he loves her by providing a home to live in or a new car to drive. She misses all of those signals.

I get it, taking out the trash is not as romantic to you as flowers and a card but it's how men show love.

Men can't handle your emotions because they don't understand them and how you express them. It's like you're speaking Greek and he's speaking English. You just aren't speaking the same language. One or both of you becomes frustrated and someone walks away angry.

If you want proof of how guys communicate, just look at a pair of six-year-old boys playing in a sandbox. Do they talk and touch each other's hair? No. They punch each other and whip sand in each other's eyes!

Your texting should be the same – punch and throw sand. Don't talk and touch his hair!

When you have a fulfilling and busy life outside of your relationship, you are less likely to be an emotional train wreck. You are constantly boosting your confidence and you don't have as great of a likelihood of getting into a codependent relationship.

Having hobbies, pursuing your passions and having a good circle of friends all helps you be in a **constant growth phase.** You're trying new things, meeting new people and not allowing your mind to go idle.

You also have options – male options!

There are a few relationship enders we need to examine before we go any further. These are things you may try, thinking you're going to put your man in his place but really, you're pushing him out of the relationship.

Many times, women deliver these relationship enders via text message. This type of message is usually too difficult to deliver face-to-face. If your guy is doing something which warrants a difficult conversation, that conversation should happen face-to-face. Most often, the type of conversation I am talking about shouldn't happen at all.

Relationship Killer #1: The Guilt Trip
If you feel the need to put someone on a guilt trip, chances are, the relationship is headed over the cliff anyway. Your guilt trip isn't going to pull it up over the edge to safety, it's going to give it the final push. Let's look at a guilt trip text:

You: What's up? What are you doing tonight?

> **Him:** Playing golf and then joining my friends to watch the Celtics game.

You: Sounds like fun. Maybe an invite next time?

> **Him:** Sure

You: Just seems like you hang out with them more than me.

The insecurity in this text sequence is about as subtle as a freight train. This guy is going to go hang out with his friends and tell them what a pain in the ass you are. You laid out your fears, being alone or left out, right there for all to see, and trust me, all will see.

This conversation makes the woman in it look terribly unattractive to her man, she lacks challenge and there is no mystery at all. There isn't anything fun or flirty about it either. Her lack of confidence is shining through.

When a woman tries to guilt a guy into doing something, his reaction, nearly 100% of the time, *if* he is a quality man, will be to do the opposite of what she is expecting. Should a quality man cave in to what the woman is demanding, he will begin to build contempt for her. The damage is being done.

For a man who is spending too much time with his friends, the answer isn't a guilt trip, it's to go do your own thing with your girlfriends. Spend time on the things you love. Stay busy, without him.

This will pique his curiosity, especially if he knows you might have an opportunity to meet a man or come across other men who may find you attractive. His sense of 'ownership' over you will kick in. Men don't like to lose their stuff and if you're dating him, you're his stuff.

I know this might sound counter-intuitive to a woman but you're getting advice from a man so I'm pretty sure it's me who is right here, not your girlfriends. For more tips on reeling in the rogue boyfriend, check out my best seller, *Who Holds the Cards Now.* This book helps women restore their power in a relationship.

Relationship Killer #2: Showing Obvious Desperation
I want you to give these needy texts a good, hard look, and then swear to me you'll never text them or anything like them to a man ever again!

- Hey, I feel like you're being distant lately.

- Why don't we hang out as much as we used to?

- Should I just assume you're seeing someone else at this point?
- Why don't you try asking me out sometime?

If you want to push your guy away, just use one of those texts. These texts reek of desperation. They are sent by a woman who wants to force her man into feeling something he doesn't feel, at least not yet. Any attempt you make to push him into showing or telling you he loves you is going to result in him running as fast as he can in the opposite direction.

Again, this is about your own insecurity and lack of confidence. These are signals to you that you need a confidence boost. It's also a signal to me that you're not busy enough. When you're busy, you don't have time to waste waiting for some guy to validate you. You're out there having fun, growing and enjoying life and meeting men.

Relationship Killer #3: He Pulls Away and You Chase
This is not a female only behavior. Both men and women do this. You sense your partner is pulling away, becoming more distant and you immediately kick it into overdrive. You start pursuing harder, spending more time trying to figure out *what's wrong*. You may catch yourself saying something like, "What did I do wrong?" or "How can I win you back?"

Forget it. This is *not* the way to reel him back in. The answer to this one is the same as the last – go do your own thing. Get busy, go take a class somewhere. Take a mini vacation or go away for the weekend with your friends. Do *something* besides beg.

Put in as much effort into him as he is putting into you… or less!

Lose the need to chase him. If you follow the guidelines in this book and he doesn't chase, then you are **done** with him. Go to option #2 or enjoy being single until option #2 arrives!

When you're texting, you should always be thinking challenge, attraction, fun, flirting and mystery. One of those, or a combination of them, should always be your goal. If you stick to that, you won't push him away with insecurity or neediness. Let's take a look:

> **You:** Pretty sure I just talked to your ex-wife at the RMV.

> **Him:** Which one?

> **You:** She didn't give me her name, I just saw her number as we waited in line.

> **Him:** If it's number 53 tell her she owes me money!

In this instance, you hooked him immediately with your first comment. Any guy will want to know what his ex is saying about him to the girl he's been hanging out with, even if his interest in her is starting to waver a bit.

He may or may not come back at you with some humor. Many times, he will demand to know what she said. In this case, play it cool and mention only vague comments like "Well, let's just say we have a lot in common!" or "She had some fun things to say about you!" or "Kidding, just screwing with you!"

If your man seems to have drifted away, it might be because you tightened the noose a little too early. If you send a text or two and he doesn't respond, wait at least a week and then start a new conversation with him in an attempt at a refresh. Whatever you make that fresh conversation about, make sure it's fun and not "Where have you been this last week."

Things you might say:

- Have you ever been to X restaurant? I just had this burger that tasted like toe jam. Stay away!

- How is it possible to stub your same toe on the same chair, twice?

These work for different reasons. What I want you to learn from them, though, is that they're light and friendly. There is no accusation, no negative emotions, just passing comments to stir his interest. If you don't come at him for this refresh in a fun, flirty and/or exciting way, he's not going to respond. He's going to think, "Here she goes again, whining about something I didn't do right." And he will roll his eyes, delete the text and move on.

If, on the other hand, your text makes him laugh or smile, you've won him back into the conversation. Stay light and friendly and let things take their natural course.

If he doesn't text you back, stop texting him and move on. You've already lost him. Your connection with him is severed and he has moved on to different pastures. This may sound harsh but I'm not here to blow sunshine up your skirt.

If you find it difficult to think of a way to reach out, think of something he likes or something you've done together in the past and see if you can stir his interest. Has he had something going on at work that you know about and can comment on in a positive, fun way? Is there a personal joke between you that you can invoke?

Look for those little things which will mean something to him and stir his desire to respond.

Chapter 4

ROMANCING BY TEXT

How do you bring romance into your texting? How do you know when to text and when to call? I know you have a lot of questions buzzing around in your head right now and I want to get them answered!

First Contact: When Should I Go For It and Should I Text or Call?

This is a question both men and women struggle with when they first meet someone new. If you text too soon, you might come off as needy but if you wait too long, he may not think you're interested. What a dilemma!

Texting has become such a common form of communication that people are often choosing it over a phone call as their initial contact method. It is not as awkward as a phone call and it's not nearly as scary for most either.

The easiest answer to this first text question is sort of a mainstay rule – wait three days. As with everything else, this is negotiable. You know yourself better so sooner might work for you, sooner being two days. Anything sooner could make you look needy and impatient. But, hey, if you have multiple options, and you don't mind the possibility of chasing him off, text him after one day.

It is okay to text him first, as long as you wait, but if you do, you need to remember the rule of keeping it fun and flirty. You want to begin building respect and attraction. Waiting three days takes the pressure off – he will probably text you within that time frame. Texting first won't make him think you're taking charge as long as you let him do so from then forward.

- Wait 2-3 days and see if he texts you
- If he doesn't, feel free to text him something witty and fun
- If you can't wait, text him using one of the examples you've read in this book.

How to "Textpress" Yourself in That First Message

If you text him first, make mention of how you met or where. Maybe you met through a friend or at a party or concert. This helps you to establish a connection with him right off. Let's check out a few examples:

> **You:** Hey it's Kerry. Quite the game!
> Sorry your team stinks, would you like
> to join my team? :-)

OR

> **You:** Hey Mister Gregg it's Laura. Had
> a blast the other night…didn't realize
> you could bring your pets to charity
> events!

Use humor and let things flow like you've known him forever. This immediately breaks the ice between you and can really get those sparks flying!

> **You:** Gotta say it…out of all the guys
> (and girls ha!) I gave my number to the
> other night you were my fav :-)

This text is fun and flattering. You land the ball in his court and give him the opportunity to respond in an equally fun and energetic way. You also injected a bit of mystery and humor by indicating you gave your number to other guys *and* girls!

Now if these texts are not you, fine, design them around your personality. I am a funny and silly type of guy so I like silly texts. You might not like my style or it doesn't fit you. The point being is to text him something unique and original.

Look it over. If another woman would text the same text – change it!

Before you send your first text, consider what you want from this guy in your relationship. Don't send a text that sends a message different from what you intend. If you're truly in it to find a guy to build a long-term relationship with, don't suggest a date for 10:00 at night. This signals more of a hookup than a nice evening out.

Remember that your texts should be building respect and value. If you want practice, practice on a man you're not interested in. Text him and see how he reacts.

Planning Dates

Avoid using general time statements like "Let's get together sometime soon" or "We'll get something set up". This tells him you're not really interested.

If he suggests a day or time that you can't make, suggest another, making sure to let him know you're excited to hear from him and go out with him. If he asks for a date on the same day, suggest another day – you should be busy.

If the date is a few days away, it doesn't hurt to send one text between when you first set up the date and when you actually go out. You can do this as a confirmation:

> **You:** I'm excited for tomorrow. Do they have apple martinis? I love apple martinis. ☺

> **Him:** I know they have the best Bombay Sapphire martini in the city. So I'd say you're in luck!

> **You:** Not good...now I'll need more than one!

> **Him:** See you at 7:00!

This is a great way to confirm a date by saying you're excited for it, and then asking him a question about it. If you had just texted "hey, we still on for tomorrow?" it sounds a bit unfriendly, almost as if you're accusing him of standing you up before you even get there. Not good!

Finally, if you don't receive a response from your first text, or the guy hasn't texted you after that week mark, I'd suggest backing off and letting that one go. Similarly, gauge the tone of his texts. They might be extremely brief, or perhaps he hasn't even mentioned going on a date with you. Maybe he's texting you at 1 a.m. asking to see you.

These are all obvious signs that he's not going to work out. Either he's simply uninterested, he's a complete jerk, or he's involved with someone else.

Don't worry if this happens! Hooking a fish and getting it into your boat are two entirely different things. Not even the experts can catch them all. You want the **right** fish, not any fish!

Texting after the First Date

While you may be excited after having a first date with a man, you want to avoid letting that excitement spill over into a text that night. It's okay to shoot him a **quick** text in the morning, but not that same night. When you send your text, focus on something specific from the night before – something fun that happened or something that really made the date worthwhile. Your morning text might go something like this:

- Awesome time last night! That blues band rocked!

- Seeing you down that fruity girly drink was a real turn on last night. ☺

- Had fun at the Topsfield fair even if wouldn't share your cotton candy!

- That was FUN! It would have been perfect if the Bruins didn't throw the game!

The last text is really effective. If you went out to a sporting event and were genuinely interested in the game he was watching, he is probably excited to see you again.

You get the drift. Stick with comments that show real interest in how things went that night. Specifics are a good way to show you care. Leave the general stuff to the women who haven't read this book – stuff like this:

- I had a great time John
- That was a lot of fun. We have to do it again sometime!
- Thanks for dinner ☺

Boring!

Pro Texting Tips

One of the ways your character shines through is in your texts. This is especially important to remember when your relationship is new. Just because you had one great date doesn't mean you have smooth sailing ahead.

There are a lot of things to learn about one another and you probably got a polished version of him, as he did of you. The real him will slowly creep through, as will the real you, over the next few dates, when you become more comfortable around one another.

Be wary of texting too much, especially early on in your relationship. You should get to know one another in person, not through texts and emails. Leave some mystery for your dates or he will mysteriously leave. On the other hand, you don't want to come off as uninterested. You will need to strike a balance and that will depend on the two of you and your individual personalities.

Men text with short bursts to their male buddies, so this is what he is most comfortable doing. Guys don't spill their guts to their guy friends – you should follow suit.

Look for patterns in his texting. Is he texting a lot? He may be clingy or insecure. Is he texting too little? He may not really be interested in continuing the relationship. Does he send boring texts? He may be a boring guy. Keep an eye on what he's sending and match this up with how he is in person.

I have some pro tips for you that will help you navigate the texting side of your relationship.

Pro Tip #1: The Automatic Responder

Wouldn't it be great if you could get him to respond right away to something you said? You could potentially use this to reignite a relationship that is flailing in the early stages, or perhaps you need a side conversation to initiate a conversation about a date.

At times like these, you want a way to get him responding immediately!

There are a few ways to do this. You can give him some information he really wants to know like:

- I read an article that I know you will love!
- Ran into someone who knows you
- This is you! Check out this video!
- Do you know anyone working at Kelly Nissan?
- I had a dream about you the other night!
- You've got some…intriguing pictures on Facebook ☺

In all of these, you've piqued his interest. You've engaged him. His ego demands that he answer! Know for sure he is wondering who you met or what you saw that caused you to mention it. When he responds, be cool and never quite tell him what or who you saw unless you want to.

Here's another way to lure him again:

> **You:** Hey check this out. I found an
> awesome article on surfing! Did you
> know there was a tournament held in
> Hawaii ever year?

> **Him:** Had no idea!
> But now I want to go!

> **You:** Well you could definitely fly
> to Hawaii. Or you could watch it at
> Encore Sports Bar with me next week
> ☺

This approach works because you are talking about something he's interested in. You have indicated that you've been paying attention and you want to know more about his likes and dislikes. Men love to be the source of knowledge for women. If you ask him a question about something he's interested in, you'll get a response.

A last approach is to prompt him to respond by teasing him.

> **You:** I saw a guy slip on ice and fall
> down getting out of his car.
> It reminded me of you landing on
> your butt after tripping over the curb
> last week!

Unless he is really uninterested in you, he is going to respond. If his interest was declining, this slight bit of teasing may jog his senses and help him see what an awesome woman you are.

Pro Tip #2: Making the Most of Emoticons

While emoticons are throughout these texting examples, they can be overused. They are powerful tools if you use them sparingly and only when they can have maximum impact.

In addition to emoticons, there are acronyms like LOL or ROFL people overuse to ensure a comment meant to be funny or sarcastic isn't taken seriously. These can be tone softeners, as can the emoticons, when you want to be sure not to offend. But please use them only on occasion. I frown when I get a LOL or a smiley face every text – it's boring!

Pro Tip #3: Give Him a Nickname

Nicknames are great! First, they can be used to tease your man remorselessly. In most cases they are slightly insulting, which puts you in a power position. Even the simple use of "Mr." before their first name is both amusing and teasing. Eventually, a nickname can become a term of endearment that mean a lot to both parties.

Feel free to recycle good nicknames for guys you meet. I enjoy using Lamb Chop—it hasn't failed me yet!

Of course, finding them can be difficult at first, but the more dates you go on with the guy, the more chances you have to come up with one. Nicknames are like Eureka moments. They pop into your head as if by magic. What I'm saying is there's no use waiting around for it. Get to know him and you'll eventually find a great one.

Pro Tip #4: Hitting the Pause Button before Sending

Just because you're typing on your phone doesn't mean you shouldn't proofread. In fact, it's probably a better case for proofing your words before you hit send. Some phones can really mess things up with autocorrect and before you know it, you've sent a completely different text than the one you intended. We've all seen the texting memes on Facebook where someone completely goes off the rails. It's funny after the fact but if you're not careful, you can offend someone.

Take time before you hit the send button to read your text. You'll be amazed at how many errors you make. Since you're only sending one at a time anyway, due to our *no double texting* rule, you've got time. This will save you tons of embarrassment and maybe even the hurt feelings of someone else.

If you are feeling highly emotional, put a pause on texting. Walk away! This is a tough time to be texting someone. Allow yourself to calm down or cool down before sending that text. You may find out that what you were emotional over isn't as bad as you thought and your text would have made things worse.

Proofing has one other benefit – you get to double check for spelling errors. Older adults especially are more in tune with the spelling and grammar of your text. They are not usually as familiar with all the texting slang and they will read your numerous typos as character flaws.

Text Etiquette

When you are on a date with Mr. Wonderful, avoid using your phone unless it's absolutely necessary. He has set aside this time in his life to be with you and you with him. You should respect his time, and yours, by giving him your full attention.

If you have children at home or you're on call for work, of course you'll have to leave it out but otherwise, put your phone away and give him your undivided attention. I'm finding older adults are getting just as bad as their kids!

If he spends half of your date texting, same rules apply – if he has kids or is on call, fine but if he's just texting his buddies about the score of the game, he's not truly interested in your date. Move on.

Common Backfire Moments: "Can I Come Back from This?"

Now, I'm not often a betting man, but if I were, I'd say that you're going to get yourself in trouble every now and then with a bad text. Either you sent something to him that you immediately regretted, or you showed yourself to be (ever so slightly) unhinged, or perhaps you simply expressed too much or too little interest.

It happens to the best of us. Dating, like everything else, is a skill we get better at with time. Of course, when you're dealing with love, it can be much harder to walk away from a mistake. But when you take it too far, taking a step back is the only way to have a chance at repairing the mistake. If you run and apologize to him you will almost never succeed!

Only apologize if you purposely run over his dog! Don't apologize if you simply said something dumb in a text. Just correct it or ignore it like it never happened.

Before we review some blunders and whether or not you can come back from them, let me say that if you find yourself making these mistakes, multiple times, it might be best to just stop contact and move on. I know that sounds harsh but these are pretty big boo-boos and your odds of keeping a guy after are slim.

You waited too long to respond and he seems uninterested...

You may seem confused by some of what you have read throughout this book. Things may seem contradictory, but really they are not. If you are following my rules, you won't allow this to happen. If a man takes 2 days to reply to you, wait 2 days to reply to him. I know this will kill you but trust me. If you wait 3 and he doesn't reply after 3-4 days, **do not** text him again. This breaks the rule of double texting, even though some time has passed.

You *might* be able to prompt him again if you wait a week and then text him again but more often than not, this doesn't work. Chances are, he lost interest in you for one reason or another.

You said the "L" word or something like it...

Both "Like" and "Love" fit into this category. Let him say these words first, otherwise you'll freak him out. If you tell him you love him first, you've shifted the balance of the relationship and he will feel pressured to either say he loves you back when he doesn't mean it, or he will bail because you got too serious too fast.

If you do make this mistake, odds are you can't recover. You need to play it cool moving forward. You have to just be patient and see if he is still interested or not.

You tried to guilt trip him into a response…
If he isn't showing you he loves you, remember he will do this through actions before he will with words, you may feel the need to pressure him to express them. **This is always a mistake.** If you do this, he will resent you and he will soon find his way to a new girlfriend.

Women have a way of using the "I don't care but really I do care" type of message. It might go something like this: "That's fine. Don't respond to me. I have better things to do anyway!" Yeah, he knows it's not fine and you aren't doing anything else but sitting there stewing over him. He's now gone and you're looking for a new guy.

It is very difficult to recover from this. This comment makes you look needy and impatient. No guy wants to date a woman like this – no quality guy anyway. Your best bet is to learn from this mistake and move on. Chances are he has already moved on anyway.

Chapter 5

TEXTING IN A NEW RELATIONSHIP

New relationships require nurturing. You don't really know one another yet and things are still easily misunderstood. You don't know his texting personality and he is unaware that you've got the patience of a 2-year-old when it comes to response times of his texts. When you are in a new relationship, the texting needs to be different than it would be if you've been dating for a while.

Think about *any* texting conversation as if it was words coming out of your mouth. How would you say it? Would you bombard the other person with sentence after sentence or would you allow them to respond? And what *if* that person said something like, "You'll have to excuse me for a while, I need to run some errands"? Would you immediately jump into a "You don't care about me" mantra or would you say, "Sure, no problem"?

When we text, we set different ground rules without realizing it and this is very difficult for a new relationship to navigate. It's important for you to remember that, even though your thumbs are doing the talking, this conversation is like any other and should be treated as such. Let's look at some new relationship texting rules you've probably broken (men too!).

The Bombardment

This is where you text him more than one or two texts at a time.

> **Lisa:** Hey Joe, what are you doing later? I thought maybe we could catch a movie.
>
> **Lisa:** *[1 hour later]* Joe????

> **Joe:** *[silent for 2 hours]* Sure, okay.

> **Lisa:** Well if you don't want to, we don't have to.

> **Joe:** It's fine. 9:00?

> **Lisa:** No, never mind. I can tell you don't want to go.
>
> **Lisa:** If you didn't want to go, all you had to do was say so.
>
> **Lisa:** I mean really, I just thought it would be nice to get together again and have some fun.

> **Lisa:** We can just talk later.
>
> **Joe:** ok

Men don't text back right away so women immediately, without fail, assume this means the man is either ignoring her or isn't interested in the conversation. While that may be true by the end of this conversation, it wasn't in the beginning. Joe was at work and couldn't answer his phone right away. Men can't multitask well. In fact, while I am writing this book I have received but not even looked at three incoming texts. I can't do both!

Rather than think of this, Lisa went on to assume he just wasn't interested in the date when he was. Of course, by the end of this conversation, he was saying "See ya sweetie you're nuts" but in the beginning, he was interested.

Be careful, when texting, not to assume feelings based on the lack of tone or lack of quantity of words, especially from men. Men and women text very differently and this is a prime example. His two to three word answers are typical male responses. He wasn't ignoring her. He wasn't being dismissive. He was texting like a man does and in the time frame men use – a couple hours, maybe even more.

Another example of bombardment is this:

Lisa: Hey I thought we could go to the movie tonight. The Rave is playing the original Star Wars movie and it sounds like fun. All I need to do is grab a shower and then I will be ready. They're showing it at 7 and 10. I was thinking we could see the 7 and then maybe grab dinner after at that little bistro down the street from the movie theater. You know, the one we walked by the other night but it was packed? Maybe they won't be so busy later in the evening.

Joe: *[doesn't respond for 2 hours]*
Okay. See you at 7.

Lisa: Well, if you don't want to go, we don't have to. Really I wish you would just tell me what you're thinking rather than making me try to guess. We can see something else or go on a different night if you don't want to see that or whatever. I'm open.

Joe: Ok, then let's go next week.

Lisa: Yeah, let's just skip it, I can tell you're not into it anyway so that's fine. I'll just stay home and read a book or something. Maybe give Fluffy a bath or watch old movies. Next time, just say you don't want to do something, you don't have to string it out all night.

Lisa: Really, it's fine. I don't mind that you're ignoring me. It's not a big deal at all. I had 3 guys ask me out just last week but I turned them down because I thought we were going out but if we're not, no biggie. I'll just call one of them. I'm sure they won't ignore me all night...no worries.

Joe: *[doesn't respond but thinks – 'see ya']*

OK, so maybe I'm exaggerating a bit to make a point but come on! Cool your heels. You wouldn't have this conversation face-to-face. Of course, the 2-hour break wouldn't have happened face-to-face either, but you need to remember that you can't see the person you're texting so you don't know *why* they're not responding.

Maybe Joe was in a big meeting with his boss or maybe he had to take his mother to the ER. Maybe he was taking a nap or driving. You don't know but your insecurity immediately jumps to the wrong conclusions and you've trashed the relationship by being impatient.

Stay on Topic

Women have this incredible knack for switching topics in the middle of a conversation. This confuses men. If you're texting him to set up a movie date, stick to the plans for that date.

> **Julie:** Hey do you want to meet me at the movie tonight or ride together?

> **Steve:** I can pick you up.

> **Julie:** Did you see that commercial for the new Star Wars movie?
> It looks good!

> **Steve:** Do you want to see that instead?

> **Julie:** No. Sara said she and John were thinking of going skiing this weekend.

> **Steve:** ??

Steve has no idea what conversation he should respond to. He thought he was making plans to pick Julie up to go see a movie but she's thrown two new topics at him without warning and he's confused. Are they going to the movie? Does she want to go skiing or go see a different movie? He's lost. Guys don't do this when they communicate. I call my friend to grab a pizza and he says, "yep, see you in 6."

Keep your conversations on topic. When you're in person, it's easier to make a topic switch without so much confusion because you're conversational partner can see the visual cues or what might have caused you to switch topics in the first place, like maybe Sara and John just walked by or you got a text from Sara letting you know about the ski trip. When you're not together and you topic hop, it just confuses the other person and makes them want out of the conversation.

Respect His Schedule

We all like to know that, when we're not with our significant other, they're at least thinking of us. This is normal. What isn't normal is to know he's on a weekend ski trip with his guy buddies and you spend the entire weekend bombarding him with texts. He's going to think you're super insecure and he's probably going to decline to respond. He doesn't want to deal with whatever hot mess those texts have turned into while he was out having fun.

Likewise, if you know he's at work, don't expect a response right away. Send something close to lunchtime if you think he might have a moment to reply. Keep things light-hearted so he doesn't have to deal with an emotional train wreck while he's trying to focus on his job.

Many men feel it is inappropriate to respond to texts while they're at work so if you get any text, you're lucky. If you do feel the need to text him while he's at work, keep things light and fun – "Hey I was just thinking again about that crazy waiter the other night." Something as simple as, "I was just thinking of you" will make him smile and remind him that he's on your mind. This is great. Men like that type of text.

The last, and perhaps most important schedule note is to be mindful of the midnight text (or later). Texting someone late at night, especially early in a relationship, can set a tone you don't want to set. If he's sleeping and you awaken him, he's not happy.

The purpose of your text can be misunderstood when it arrives late at night as well. He might think you want to hook up – that you're sending a booty call text. If you want a real, serious relationship with this guy, a late-night text can cause significant damage in how he views you. It could make him think you have no boundaries and he could begin to see you as a rest stop, not a keeper.

Keep Things Positive

This is a big one and something I gauge a woman on. It's easy to share your frustrations and anger via texting but avoid doing this with your man – especially early in your relationship. You want your early communication with him to be positive and uplifting, not to make you look like Debbie Downer. Even if your boss just hacked you off and you're ready to strangle someone, texting it to your new beau is not the right venue for your frustration.

When you present negativity to a new guy, it becomes the first few notes of the death knell of your relationship. No man wants to be with a woman who is always negative. Even if it's just a complaint about how your mom always has to call and check up on you, it's negative and best left for a time when you can say it and laugh about it, rather than send it without any tone behind it.

If you feel the need to share the negatives of your day, do so with your girlfriends. Get it all off of your chest now, before you text or go on a date with him. He will appreciate you getting rid of all of that before he sees you! Chances are, if you're being negative, you're also highly emotional. He can't handle this, nor does he want to.

Remember, this guy is still getting to know you. Whether it's a text or in person, you need to put your best foot forward. Keep texts fun and flirty or complimentary. "I really liked how you made our waiter laugh last night" or "I thought it was great how you talked to that little girl in the park who had lost her dog". Let him know you're enjoying his company. Boost his ego a little. Remind him he's on your mind. All okay!

Always Tell Me Good Night

You've probably seen this on a pillow or a sign some-where – maybe you've even got it hanging up in your home somewhere: *"Always kiss me good night"*. Well, this goes for texting too. The two favorite texts men *do* like to receive are "Good Morning" and "Good Night". It's nice to know you are the first person someone thinks about when they awaken and the last person they think about before they go to sleep.

Men, in particular, have expressed a strong like for these two texts. They're simple but they convey an important message to them – "I'm thinking of you".

Now, the trick for you is not to expect a response. Sure, he may come back with "Good morning" or "Good night" as well, and that's great, but if he doesn't, chill. It may mean he's already up and at it or he's already asleep for the night. Don't bombard him because he didn't reply. His lack of response also doesn't mean he didn't enjoy seeing those texts. Of course, this is not done until you have built a rapport.

Chapter 6

THE 10 RULES OF ENGAGEMENT

Women always wonder if there are 'rules' to texting men. Well, there are and it's important that you become aware of them because odds are, you're breaking some of them. Here is quick cheat sheet to review.

Rule 1: Never send more than 3 unanswered texts

We covered bombarding texts in Chapter 1, but this is not something limited to early in a relationship. You should never send a guy (or anyone for that matter) more than 3 texts that go unanswered. At the same time you're limiting your texts to 3 unanswered, don't become impatient that your texts are unanswered. Be patient. He will reply and if he doesn't, he isn't into you or he got eaten by a shark. Either way, move on.

Rule 2: Save the emoticons

Unless you're a teenager, emoticons are not for relationships, generally speaking. As you get to know someone, you may sneak in one or two, but keep their use to a minimum. Sending a string of laughing-out-loud faces is fine if he just told you something that really cracked you up but save the cute stuff for your girlfriends. As your relationship advances, there may be a few that you use between you and that's fine. Generally speaking, though, these are severely overused.

Rule 3: Use sentences – ditch the abbreviations

The days of 'wat r u dng ths wknd?' are over. Talk and text like an adult who knows how to spell and use grammar. If a man has to spend too much time trying to decode your text, he will probably just give up and ignore the whole conversation. A grown man expects you to text like a grown woman who can carry on a conversation.

Rule 4: Playing hard to get is okay – to a point

You need to gauge this one, based on the guy you're dating. Some men are really turned off by this game. They see it for what it is – an attempt to make him work for it – and they just don't want to take the time to play. Other men see this as the thrill of the chase deal and they're excited by it.

Know which type of man you are dating! My best seller *Manimals* will teach which type of man you are dealing with and how best to engage him.

If your guy seems to be a more direct, to the point kind of guy, he probably isn't going to be into the 'hard to get' game so don't bother with it. The 'sensitive man' falls into this category. If, on the other hand, he seems excited by you and is enjoying chasing you, by all means, give him a little hard to get now and then.

When you're playing hard to get in texts, you're probably just texting like a guy would – meaning you wait a little while to respond to his inquiry and you tease. Again, if your guy is more direct and he responds to you quickly, you want to respond in kind and not mess around.

Rule 5: Once a day to say 'hey' is plenty

Don't come off as needy. You can send one text in a day to say 'hey' but that's it. Any more and you're coming off as being too demanding or needy. And, while you're at it, 'hey' isn't terribly original. Try "Thinking of you Babe" or "Did you kick butt at your presentation?" or even "Why do squirrels purposely run under my tires?" kind of stuff shows you care (even about squirrels) and is more engaging. You want to let him know you're thinking of him without pushing him away.

Rule 6: Texting first is okay – but

It's nice to show someone you're interested in them, so men don't mind if you text first, however, if he doesn't respond for one reason or another, let it go. Especially early in a relationship, things can be a bit foggy about whether or not he's interested. If he doesn't seem to be responding to your texts, he's just not that into you. Don't take offense or bombard him with mean or ugly texts. Just move on.

Rule 7: Don't drunk text – just don't

Everyone has sent and received this text. The rule is just don't do it. When you drink, your inhibitions are lowered. Any boundaries you may have successfully set can be eliminated and your reputation as a keeper can be tossed out the window pretty quickly. Texts are more emotional when you're drunk. Men can't handle 'emotional', whether it's in a text or otherwise. If you're out drinking with your girlfriends and you feel the urge to text him, resist and chat with them instead. He won't miss your text if you don't send it, but if you send something too far over the edge, you could push him away for good.

Rule 8: Know your audience

Not all men are texters – not all people are texters. The older you are, the more this may be true. It's important for you to get a read on whether or not your guy even likes to text. If you're an older couple, your guy may be more old school and may prefer a phone call. Calls are more intimate and the tone of your voice is easier to detect. Men are visual so hearing your voice may stir in him a vision of something you said or the way you smile when you say certain things. He may hear your laugh and remember how your eyes light up when you laugh. Don't demand texting of a man who isn't into it.

Rule 9: Keep it brief

In case you haven't noticed, men aren't big on words, whether it's in a text or in person. Women, on the other hand, seem to have an endless supply. The trick to successfully texting *with* a man is to text *like* a man. This means you use short, to the point texts, at least until you get to know him and what he will tolerate. Generally speaking, men are two to three word texters with the occasional sentence thrown in. They don't like abbreviations or slang and will gauge you on how well you spell, use grammar and punctuation. He doesn't want your life story in text. Save that for a date when he's excited to talk to you. Use texting to set up that date or remind him he's been on your mind.

Rule 10: Keep your expectations reasonable

In new relationships in particular, we get excited about the new person, but we're also nervous. Does he really like me? Did I push him away with that story about the jellyfish? And on and on. Men get nervous too but, the difference is we won't bombard you with texts to resolve it. Try to keep your expectations reasonable when it comes to texting. You've got the previous 9 rules to follow and most of them, if you follow them, will help you follow this rule as well. Don't expect him to be able to text you cute little smileys while he's at work, and especially if he's out with his friends. Allow things to flow naturally and let the texts enhance how your relationship progresses.

Chapter 7

IS TEXTING HEALTHY IN RELATIONSHIPS?

You may or may not be wondering if texting is even a good thing for your relationship. The easy answer is, it depends on your age and how into texting the two of you are. The longer answer is that there are definite benefits and pitfalls.

Here are the advantages and disadvantages:

ADVANTAGES

Let's start with the positive first. There are a few advantages to texting in relationships, far fewer advantages than disadvantages, but still, they exist. Let's learn how to use them to your advantage.

Texting doesn't require you to be fast on your feet

If you're one of those people who thinks of a good comeback 10 minutes later, texting could be a great avenue for you. When you're one-on-one with someone and they say something witty, you may be expected to come up with your own clever response right away. When you're texting this conversation, you've got plenty of time to be clever. The great thing is that a man won't notice the time lapse and he will appreciate the humor when it is delivered.

Your jitters are all yours

You met this guy last night at the book signing after work and you really liked him. Now you'd like to shoot him a text, just to say you enjoyed meeting him, but you're a nervous wreck. Your hands are shaking and you're perspiring like crazy. He'll never know and that's the great thing about this text. All of your nerves and jitters will be hidden behind your well-put-together text (which leads us to the next advantage).

You can think through your response

When you are having a conversation via text, you have time to formulate a great response. You can take some time to think through exactly what you want to say and make sure your spelling and grammar are perfect. You can't go backwards and take back spoken words, so this is a definite advantage!

You can use synchronicity to your advantage

If you're paying close attention, you can quickly pick up on his texting style and mimic it. This helps to create a feeling of similarity or synchronicity. In my best seller, *Night Moves*, I talk about how using synchronicity can help a guy feel as if he's falling in love with you. One of the first and easiest ways you can do this is to pick up his texting style and repeat it back to him. Powerful stuff indeed!

You can flirt a little

You don't want to get down and dirty in texts, especially early on in a relationship, but you can flirt and keep the excitement alive in between dates. We've already talked about how you don't need to bombard him with texts all day or send more than one 'thinking of you' type of text in a day, but if worded properly, one will do the trick. We'll talk more about flirting in texts later but for now, know that it's a great way to keep things a little exciting without being trashy.

You can remind him you're thinking of him

Men do like this 'thinking of you' text as you've read. It's a nice way to let him know this without becoming too intrusive in his day. If you use this as part of your 'good morning' text, even better.

You can acknowledge a message

If you're busy, in a meeting, or otherwise occupied and your guy calls, a quick text to say, "Hey I got your message and I'll call you later" lets him know you're not ignoring him but you can't talk right now. This is a great way to divert the conversation until a time when you can talk.

You can stay in touch when traveling

This is especially true if you're overseas. You can send a text, even internationally, for basically free to let your guy know he's on your mind. This can be a big deal when you're away for a while or your relationship is new and you want him to know he's not forgotten.

DISADVANTAGES

While there are a few advantages to texting in relationships, there are far more disadvantages. I'm not saying this should dissuade you from texting in *your* relationship, but I want you to be aware of the pitfalls so you can avoid them. Many times, simply changing your method or wording can help you avoid these.

All emotion and tone is lost

The obvious first disadvantage of texting in a relationship is one we've already mentioned. In a text, you cannot decipher the tone of someone's voice or the emotion behind their message. This leaves you open to misunderstandings that can be relationship killers. Yes, this is where an emoticon can be a difference maker, but remember, we said to use those sparingly.

If one or both of you are shy...

Texting can easily replace face-to-face conversations if one or both of you are shy. This can lead you down a road to having a text only conversation which will ultimately end your relationship. Even if you're shy, you need face time with your guy. Be sure to keep a balance of a little bit of texting and more time talking, even if it's on the phone, it is better than texting *all* of the time.

Too much texting killed the couple

Couples who reported heavy texting in their relationship, also report a higher level of dissatisfaction with that relationship. Why? Because no intimacy can be built through texting. Intimacy is built by doing things together and building memories. I call these *putting pennies in the jar* and those pennies do not transfer through phones.

Over analysis paralysis

It's easy to spend too much time analyzing what the other person said. A text that is confusing can be misunderstood and then the over analyzing begins. Women are particularly good at this, "What do you think he meant by *this???*" As with many of the other texting pitfalls, this can be especially true early in a relationship when you don't know one another very well. You don't know what he meant, so rather than ask, you guess and usually, you guess wrong.

We label each other – incorrectly

We naturally label people. It's human nature. The problem with this behavior is that we're usually wrong. When you text in a certain way, you're likely to be labeled. If your grammar is poor or you choose not to take the time to spell things properly, he will label you as less than mature. If you want to direct his label of you, be careful how, when and what you text.

It can be endless

Have you ever gotten caught up in one of those texting conversations where it seems as if it never ends? This is a real pitfall of texting. Where does it end? On the one hand, your conversations need to be natural, but on the other hand, there does need to be a point when the 'too much texting' agony will be over. Be careful not to make your conversations endless and meaningless. Be the first to stop.

Absence can make the heart grow colder

Men will use texting in a relationship to distance themselves from the relationship. If you notice your guy seems to be texting more or pulling back, he could be using the lack of personal contact to remove himself from your relationship. Is it a crappy way to end things? Yep, but it's possible that's just what he's doing.

Anything you say can be held against you

It's key to remember that the words you text are perma-nent. If you are married, for example, your texts could be called into play in a divorce situation. Additionally, any sexting or other texts you send which are less than hon-orable could come back to haunt you in the future. You cannot control what happens to your text when it reaches the other person's phone. Remember this and never send anything you wouldn't want to see again in a legal battle or on social media.

You can be someone else – and so can he

When your relationship relies too heavily on texting, you can be another version of yourself. You can be funnier and more relaxed or some other version of yourself. While this seems great on the surface, eventually you need to meet the person you're in a relationship with and the real you will come out. By the same token, your guy can be pretending to be someone or something he isn't. The big-gest danger here is when you meet someone online and you've never met in person. This persona either of you creates can't last forever and when the truth comes out, chances are your relationship, for whatever it was worth, will be over.

Madame Editor

As we've discussed previously, texts can be edited, thought about, planned. This means you may not be sending the *real* version of yourself. When you are speaking to some-one, either face-to-face or on the phone, your words are more spontaneous and less planned. You are a truer ver-sion of yourself. Be aware that he too can edit and rewrite his texts.

You're just stuck

A text-based relationship is likely to get stuck in a place it can't recover from. Texting conversations are less inti-mate because you're not together, face-to-face, sharing the experience and the atmosphere around you. The texts are not as deep or meaningful and there is no emotion. This text-heavy relationship will get stuck at some point because there is no real depth or emotion between you. You may think your conversations are deep or thought-ful, but they cannot be without the body language and facial expressions which make conversation meaningful and emotional.

Chapter 8

WHAT MEN DO AND DON'T WANT TO SEE

Men do enjoy hearing from you but there are things they do and do not want to see in a text. The texting side of your relationship should be balanced. What I mean by this is you should not send more than you receive and vice versa. The person sending more than he or she receives is the one who will come off as needy and maybe impatient. You don't want to be that person and if *he* is that person, you want to move on. There are things men do like to see in the messages they receive so let's focus on that.

What He Wants to See

Kill Him with Kindness

Who doesn't enjoy a little flattery? Men sure do! If you want to just shoot him a text to let him know you're thinking of him, great! All I ask is that you throw in something meaningful. Let's look at a few examples:

- I really enjoyed how you thanked the veteran for his services and paid for his coffee – that was wonderful!

- That was a memorable time last night! I now enjoy jazz - his voice was awesome!!! Great idea!

- That bistro you chose for dinner was oh so tasty! Take me back!

- I'm still laughing at the waiter joke you told me last night!

These texts all deliver a compliment and give your man a little ego boost. That's always a good thing. When you send a text like this, however, I want you to be sure not to expect or demand a response. He saw your text and it made him smile. He will respond at some point but don't be surprised if it isn't immediately.

Make It Fun!

Nobody wants to read a text that turns out to be a real buzz kill! Keep your texts light and fun. This is the one place where using an emoticon might be to your advantage. Putting a smiley at the beginning of a text is an automatic signal that fun is on the way! There are several ways in which you can inject fun into your texts.

- Use a meme that you know will be meaningful to him – maybe it relates to a personal joke between the two of you or maybe it reminds you both of something fun you did together

- If you share a love of something, like sports, interject something like this, "Hey that date was great except when the Cavaliers lost the game – then I hated you! ☺ "

- If you've been dating for a while, give him a pet name, one that has meaning to both of you, and use it occasionally in your texts

Flirt but Not in an Obvious Way

Men have vivid imaginations and flirting in a text message is a great way to stir his, but you want to be careful not to give away the whole store. Subtlety in flirty texts is your best weapon. Let his imagination take care of the rest. All you need to do is toss something out there.

For example, if he asks what you're doing, you can say something like, "Just got out of the shower" or "Changing my clothes" and his mind is off and running. Whether he's seen you naked or not, he's got this one covered.

An Invitation

"Hey I saw on Facebook that The Pub is showing the Knicks game on Saturday. Can you join me?" If your guy loves the Knicks, chances are he's in. Inviting a guy on a date is okay to do if you do it like this – sort of a back-handed way. Generally speaking, you want to allow him to take charge but what you're saying is. "*I'm already planning to be there if you want to tag along*". This is a less formal 'date' than if you planned dinner together at a fancy restaurant.

You can also try something like, "Hey I am ordering wings from that place on 5th that we both liked so much. Want some?" Again, you're already doing something, whether he joins or not, you're just including him if he chooses. He may say yes or he may already have plans, but either way, he will enjoy the text.

One caveat with this type of text. If you're inviting him to your place, make sure you set the agenda or he might presume you want to have sex. "I'm watching the Celtics on my new TV tomorrow night. Care to join me?" sets the tone – you're inviting him over to watch the game.

Good Morning or Good Night

Nothing beats knowing you're the first thing someone thinks about when they rise or the last thing they think about before they go to sleep. Men are no exception. Sending a simple, "Good Morning" is great as long as you don't turn it into an all-day exchange. Send it and move on. No need for him to reply, but if he *does*, let it go at that. Remember – let him text last! Allow his reply to be the end of that conversation.

Cheeky but Fun Facts About You

Men love mystery and when you present odd little facts about yourself that are interesting, it piques his interest. "Hey, did you know I'm a huge fan of classic cars? I need someone to help me decide which one to buy." is a fun fact and an off-hand invitation. Double good.

You can feed him little facts about you in this way. These are great conversation starters for your next date too, especially if it's something he's also interested in. "I was thinking about going hiking this weekend. Have you ever gone to ..." He may not have realized you were into hiking and now he wants to know more!

I Love You

This one comes with a warning. This is a text for much later in your relationship, after this has been said by him, then you, in person. **Never** be the first to say "I love you", and **never ever** say it for the first time in a text. This is an especially intimate moment between the two of you and it will be something you always remember. Don't make that memory a screen shot.

What He Doesn't Want to See From You

Men don't want to see many things in a text. Remember, your mantra should be *"Catch me if you can"* when you compose a text. If your text doesn't conjure up that feeling, it's probably not a good one to send. Let's review some texts you should never send a guy.

The Apology Text

Never apologize in a text. If you sent a text you regret, you need to apologize in person or at least on the phone. Texting is not the place for an apology. It seems insincere and he'll probably ignore it.

The other danger of apologies is using them too much. Some people are apologizers. What this really means is that they're approval seeking, which is a sign of low confidence. You want to make sure you don't say things like "I'm sorry" or "Just kidding" in texts. They both mean the same thing, *"Hey take back those words I just sent that you will be able to see forever, I didn't mean them"*.

Many times, especially when we text, we think the other person may misconstrue the text we sent, so we feel the need to apologize. Rather than assume he got angry, wait and see. If you meant your text to be a bit of a tease, stick in a smile emoticon to let him know it's all in fun. While I did say not to use emoticons often, there is definitely a time and place for them, and softening the blow of your words is one example.

Slang and Abbreviations

You're a grown up. At work, you write in full sentences with punctuation. The same grammar and spelling rules apply in texting. Avoid using 'wut' for 'what' and 'idk' for 'I don't know' types of substitutions. Using a ton of these in a text is not only immature but it is difficult to read, especially if someone isn't a proficient texter. Use real words spelled correctly and all will be well with your messages.

Nude Photos of You

Please, *please* do not sext, or send someone nude photos of yourself. As I mentioned previously, men are visual so they like hints of what you're up to, not the real photo. Aside from that, once you send this type of photo, it is out of your control. You send it to him, he goes out with his buddies and has one too many, shows his buddies the text or maybe even sends it to a few friends, then, it ends up on social media. Bam. Your reputation is ruined.

This can also play out this way. You sext him, a few weeks later, you break up with him. He goes online and finds a site for photos of ex-girlfriends, posts your nude photos and bingo, you're out there for all to see. And I might mention that "all" could be your current or potential employers, clients, children, parents, or siblings. Always remember that once it's gone past your own phone, it's out of your control.

Emotional Texts

Save your emotional texts for your girlfriends. Guys don't want to see or hear your high emotion. They really don't know what to do with it. It always reminds me of the first episode of *Big Bang Theory* when the boys first meet the pretty girl, who starts crying after a few moments. One mouths to the other, "What do we do?" and the other shrugs his shoulders. Geeky boys aren't the only ones clueless about female emotions, all men shrug their shoulders.

Keep your texts fun and exciting. You want to be building respect and attraction, not resentment.

A Book

Nobody wants to read a book of a text. What I mean by this is those texts where you have to scroll the screen to read the whole thing. I mention this in the 'texting in a new relationship chapter' and call it bombardment. Men like as few words as possible while still conveying the message. This doesn't mean you limit yourself to 4 words always, but it does mean that you avoid the screen-filling text at all cost. If you have that much to say, you need to talk either on the phone or in person.

Dismissive Texts

If he is texting you, he's interested in you. When you respond with "K" or "Cool" or "Great", it's dismissive. Even texts like, "Sounds good" leave him thinking you're not really interested in the conversation. If you don't have the time to send an appropriate text at that moment, write it a little later when you can take the time to respond properly. If you won't be able to respond for a while, shoot him a quick text that says, "Hey I'm buried at work right now but I will definitely get back to you later tonight."

A Guilt Trip

Please, please don't throw a guilt trip on your guy in a text message. We talked about this already but it's worth a reminder. Guilt trips come in the form of complaint, "You always spend so much time with your friends" or "I hate that you never remember to text me that you arrived safe". This type of text screams of insecurity and guys hate it. It shows him that your confidence isn't very high and will make him want out.

Rather than deliver a guilt trip, go do your own thing with your own friends. If he gets to see how hot you look before you leave, bonus! Let him know that, while he's out watching basketball with his buddies, you'll be out having wine with your girlfriends. He will spend at least half of the game wondering if other guys are seeing you, approaching you, interested in you. He may even shoot you a text or two while you're out. It's driving him crazy. Because you didn't whine and complain about him being out, and instead showed him you can go out too, he will likely decrease his time he spends with his buds.

Just Remember

If you simply remember to keep things fun and exciting, you won't have any problems. Be brief and allow his imagination to take over if you're flirting with him.

CONCLUSION

You have learned a lot about texting men. You've learned how to understand why he texts you back two hours after you send a message, and why he texts back with three or four words.

Most importantly, you've learned the mantra with which you should always text – *catch me if you can*. If you remember this when you're texting, you will be sending him messages that intrigue him, challenge him and help him feel attracted to you! All win-win texts!

When you create attraction, desire, mystery and challenge, you're drawing him closer to you *and* you are increasing the chances of him responding to your text faster. Men need this challenge – they need to feel as if they're chasing. It's what keeps a guy interested in you.

Guys are built to pursue women. It's in our DNA. This holds true for all ages. Heck, a mid-life crisis is just an older man who has gone unchallenged for too long and is bored. It only makes sense that your texting needs to create a challenge for him, especially in the early going.

You want short, fun and challenging interactions. Be bold, quirky, funny and direct! Forget the boring stuff and show him your flirty side. You have tons of time to figure out a response, so relax and wait for it to come!

And remember, the key to great texting is often what you don't text! Fight the urge to text long paragraphs and send messages like, "How is your day going?" Avoid the message string that won't go anywhere. Don't get caught up in a 'tell me all about your day' type of sequence. He will quickly get bored with it and stop replying.

Instead, talk about your day in person. Delay and vary your texts, let him be the last to text, and keep things pithy so he is curious and excited to see what else you are capable of!

Thank you for joining me in my quest to make you awesome!!

Gregg

AUTHOR BIO

As one of Boston's top dating coaches, my books rest prominently atop the dating advice genre. In my role as a life coach, I've been known to be unorthodox, in a good way, and I break a few rules. I assist both men and women and help them understand one another.

I won't bore you with my professional bio. Instead, I will share with you the story of how I became a dating and life coach and what makes me qualified to coach you.

The irony of my story is that I come from an extremely dysfunctional family. I witnessed the marriage of my parents crumble before my eyes at an early age. Flying dishes seemed normal in my household. I came out a bit angry and I have 12 years of failed relationships to show for it.

Fortunately, I started encountering positive things in my life. I discovered that couple, that elusive, elderly couple still holding hands in the park at the ripe old age of eighty. They gave me hope. As a problem solver, I could solve anything...except relationships, damn it!

I couldn't figure out why my folks represented the norm rather than the exception to married life. Fifty-five percent of all marriages end in divorce. Why? "What is wrong?"

In 2009, after a long stretch of living the single life, I had an epiphany. I attended a Christmas show at my Dad's church. I am not a religious person, but when I saw the cheerful couples and witnessed the powerful music, I was touched. I needed answers to love and I wanted true love for myself.

I was tired of my shallow single life. I decided to study my failures and interview as many single people and couples as I could. I even watched the movie, Hitch, and it motivated me to help others.

I realized I possessed a natural ability to help others discover love, and knew it was my future. Can you guess where I started? Yep, those happy elderly couples. Sure, I got maced a few times as I approached them with questions, but the knowledge I gained was priceless!

Since then, I have met thousands of people: happy couples, unhappy couples, single people of all types, and everything in between. I quickly learned that confidence played a large role in both attracting and keeping a partner.

My friends encouraged me to launch a dating advice website. I now own the top dating site for women, *Who Holds the Cards Now.*

Men and women contact me after reading my books. I have become a "Dear Abby" of sorts. Today, after thousands of interviews, I have accomplished my goal. I broke the code and enjoy a great relationship myself. Now I plan to share my findings with **you**!

I have come to realize that even though people believe what I teach, they still suffer a serious problem. They lack the motivation and confidence to execute my tactics. A course change was required. I started concentrating on life coaching in addition to my date coaching. If you can't love yourself, how can you love someone else? It's impossible.

Now, I concentrate on pulling people in and guiding them to understanding themselves. I assist them in creating clarity in their lives, setting goals, and creating the path to attain those goals. I offer inspiration, passion, and spirituality with the constant live like you're dying attitude. People are transformed through my books and daily exercises.

I have written many Amazon Best Sellers, several of which reached #1 Best Seller status. Together we can build your confidence, increase your self-esteem, and propel you closer to your goals.

You will discover happiness by completing the work most people will never attempt!

Today, I travel and teach in all the sexy playgrounds: LA, South Beach, and Las Vegas. I can help you in your journey to find love and build confidence so we can transform your life.

I am not merely a best-selling author, my readers are my friends and I communicate with them directly. I humbly ask you to allow me to help you. Join me on my quest for your happiness, your exciting journey to an extraordinary life!

Gregg Michaelsen, Confidence Builder

I feel you need two very important skills before you start dating again: confidence in yourself and an understanding of the male mind. I provide both because I am a life coach and a male dating coach. I have two rockin' paid courses with tons of videos featuring me if you're interested.

Understand men: *who-holds-the-cards-now.thinkific.com/ courses/the-man-whisperer*
Find confidence: *who-holds-the-cards-now.thinkific.com/ courses/build-yourself-and-he-will-come/*

GET THE WORD OUT TO YOUR FRIENDS

If you believe your friends would draw something valuable from this book, I'd be honored if you'd share your thoughts with them. If you feel particularly strong about the contributions this book made to your success, I'd be eternally grateful if you would post a review on Amazon. You can check them out by visiting the links below. My coed motivational books are listed after the women's books.

Women's Dating Advice Books

Please read the jewel of all my books: *To Date a Man, You Must Understand a Man.* This companion book to all my books will help you understand men! Read the hundreds of reviews to learn how well my tactics work! Another #1 best seller.

Next, take understanding men to another level with *10 Secrets You Need to Know About Men.*

If you want to make sure you don't get played, you need to read *Weed Out The Users, The Couch Potatoes and The Losers*

One of my latest books is selling like crazy!
Pennies in the Jar: How to Keep a Man for Life is the ultimate women's guide to keeping a relationship strong!

More Awesome Best Sellers to Solve Your Dating Issues!

Would you like to make a man fall in love with you?
Try *Night Moves*!

If you're single and looking? Read *The Social Tigress*.

Do you want to learn more about men?
Read *Manimals: Understanding Different Types of Men and How to Date Them*.

Are you ready for a serious change?
Read *Own Your Tomorrow*.

Do you want to text a man into submission?
#1 Best Seller: *Power Texting Men*.

Would you like to take yourself on a self-discovery journey?
Read *To Date a Man You Must Understand Yourself*.

Have you just gone through a breakup? Gain an in-depth understanding of what your mind and body are going through with *He's Gone, Now What?*

Do you want your ex back? I'll give you your best chance with *How to Get Your Ex Back Fast*.

If you want to regain control of your relationship, try *Who Holds the Cards Now?*.

Confidence attracts!
Get it here: *Comfortable in Your Own Shoes*.

Would you like to clean up online?
Read *Love is in The Mouse* & *Love is in the Mouse 2017*.

Are you over 40 and getting back into the dating scene?
Check out *Middle Aged and Kickin' It*.

Are you in need of some introvert dating help?
Take a peek at *Be Quiet and Date Me!*.

Need help in your long distance relationship?
Committed to Love, Separated by Distance.

Books for Men and Women that Motivate!

Live Like You're Dying

The Power to Communicate

I can be reached at *Gregg@WhoHoldsTheCardsNow.com.*

Please visit my website just for women,
Who Holds the Cards Now.

Facebook: *WhoHoldsTheCardsNow*
Twitter: *@YouHoldTheCards*
I'm a Your Tango Expert

You are my motivation!

Gregg

Made in the USA
Columbia, SC
29 June 2019